LEVERAGING YOUR LINKEDIN PROFILE FOR SUCCESS

Maximizing Your Exposure and Achieving Verified Results

MATTHEW T. FRITZ

ISBN: 1500818100
ISBN-13: 978-1500818104

DEDICATION

This book is dedicated to seekers and communicators everywhere who are longing for a way to make connections, expand their networks and create new conversations. It is my hope that this text provides value and insight, as well as new ideas. My inspiration has been my family, who has pushed, prodded and cajoled me to put these words on paper and share them with you—my newest connection!

LEVERAGING YOUR
LINKEDIN PROFILE
FOR SUCCESS

MAXIMIZING YOUR EXPOSURE
AND ACHIEVING VERIFIED RESULTS

MATTHEW T. FRITZ

CONTENTS

WELCOME

As a user of LinkedIn since 2003, I've enjoyed the many benefits of this social-media networking tool and have experienced great success in making professional contacts that have paid valuable dividends. The beauty of LinkedIn is that the tool is easily accessible and the benefits are available to anybody who takes the time to find and utilize them. I am confident that with a bit of time and energy, you can receive the same kind of value and exceed your expectations. It all starts with a desire to get out there and explore.

Whether you are dipping your toe into the waters of LinkedIn or you have had a long-established profile with them, the fact you are reading this means you are interested in capitalizing upon LinkedIn's capabilities for maximum effect. Congratulations—you are among the 3% of LinkedIn users who have made a conscious choice to do so! As a result, you stand to reap significant rewards for your efforts—as standing out among your peers is what LinkedIn is all about.

Over the next few pages, I will share my views on the benefits of LinkedIn's offering and how you can leverage them to your advantage. This wonderful social-media platform holds a treasure-trove of opportunities for those who understand and utilize these capabilities properly. Through a systematic breakdown of the elements in your profile, as well as an exploration of other forums and capabilities within LinkedIn, my goal is for you to have all the tools you need to take full advantage of this medium.

I look forward to sharing my insights with you and helping you to receive the same benefits I have enjoyed. What awaits you is the opportunity to make connections with like-minded individuals far beyond your current networking capabilities. Through these contacts, you can engage and interact across business barriers and cultural divides to achieve your goals. The greatest gift of technology is communication, and LinkedIn provides a unique and established way of igniting conversations. Let's keep the conversation going!

Matthew T. Fritz
LinkedIn.com/in/fritzmt

LOOK FOR THE BONUS SYMBOL TO TAKE
ADVANTAGE OF LITTLE-KNOWN CAPABILITIES!

1 ABOUT LINKEDIN

LinkedIn is a professional networking site, which debuted in 2002, and went public in 2011. It has become the professional network of choice for more than 225 million members and grows by almost two new members per second. It is the professional equivalent of the old game "Six Degrees of Kevin Bacon." For instance, you may want to work in a particular field—but don't know anybody in this particular field. Chances are, however, that you know someone who knows someone in that particular field. Through LinkedIn, you are capable of making contact—through your professional network—with the people you want to contact. In the process, you can potentially gain the endorsement and recommendations of people

WHY LINKEDIN?

LinkedIn is more than a social-media venue—it is a part of your professional toolbox. With so many businesses and individuals searching for faster and better ways to comprehensively scan large pools of people to find "the right fit" for their need—whether that be hiring, partnerships, mentors, customers or suppliers—LinkedIn stands out as one of the most widely-used initial screening points. For that matter, LinkedIn provides you a "foot in the door" for the next step in the conversation. Researchers take the form of CEOs, Human Resources departments, members of the media, bosses, potential customers, future partners, future neighbors and current friends. Failing to catch the attention of a researcher in their first wide-cast and initial scan can result in a degraded relationship before it even starts. This can translate into lost jobs, lost business and lost opportunities. In a world where so much information is no further than your nearest computer or tablet screen, can you afford not to take advantage of LinkedIn?

WHAT IS IT ALL ABOUT?

Like any successful social-media platform, LinkedIn brings a variety of offerings to its customers in an attempt to satisfy a variety of needs. At the most basic level, it provides individuals the opportunity to construct a profile that tells their story. It then provides everybody the ability to search their database of individuals based upon keywords (see "About Keywords") which fit their search criteria. However, the fun doesn't end there—LinkedIn offers so much more. Organizations have the ability to create "Company Pages" which allow them to showcase their unique offerings and allow individuals to affiliate themselves to the organization. Through company pages, organizations can even post available job opportunities and leverage the vast network of individuals to seek good matches. Notice we haven't really even broached the social-media aspect yet—having merely touched upon the billboard functions provided by LinkedIn.

Individuals have the ability to communicate via LinkedIn's networking system. Networking starts when an individual selects another individual and makes an offer for a connection. The receiving individual has the option to accept that request from the sender to join their network, thereby establishing a 1st-degree connection relationship. Once two individuals are connected, they can view the members of each other's networks and attempt to make network connections with them. Making a connection with a member of a 1st-degree connection's network would be called a 2nd-degree connection. Once contact is made with a 2nd-degree network member and they accept the networking request, they are directly connected and become a 1st-degree connection, just as the original member through with the connection is made.

The real power of LinkedIn comes in the form of 3rd-degree network connections. Reaching out to a 3rd-degree connection—that is, someone who is not directly connected to you or to your direct 1st-degree connections—requires use of a special capability within LinkedIn called an introduction. Through an introduction, you make a request to "meet" or be "introduced" to an individual who isn't currently in reach. Much like real life, the person you contact for an introduction has the option to help or not—and if they do help, they are essentially vouching for you in the process. Another way to make this connection would be through an "InMail," which is LinkedIn's special way of circumventing the introduction process for those individuals you want to contact directly who may be either completely out of your network, or only tangential, at best. In LinkedIn's own words, an InMail is a professional, credible outreach with your profile attached that doesn't' require an introduction.

Now the business model comes into play. LinkedIn only allows so many introductions and InMails per user and how many you have available to you depends upon your membership level. LinkedIn offers premium subscription plans for job seekers, businesses, and recruiters, which allow introductions in excess of the five offered to basic (free) members. As well, premium users are allowed to view open profiles, receive InMail bonuses, and access premium search features. Another interesting feature offered to premium members is the ability to see who has looked at them in a level of detail much higher than basic (free) members. This can be useful when making reverse-connections with folks who may have peeked, but not taken the opportunity reach out and make the connection with you themselves. At the time of writing, LinkedIn Premium plans start at $19.99/month billed annually for basic job-seekers and sales-professionals and rise as high as $719.95/month for corporate recruiters. In many cases, after some time and at a point of advanced profile building, basic members will receive an enticing email from LinkedIn offering a free 30-day trial of premium membership to experiment with features and decide whether a longer-term premium membership is right for them.

On top of all of these capabilities, LinkedIn also offers other connection opportunities through an organic messaging system, interesting articles you can read and interact through, endorsements, and invitations. All of this is made available based upon the highly customizable privacy settings built into each user's control panel. In essence, you can share as much as you like and allow as much contact as you are comfortable with. In the end, using LinkedIn effectively is about maximizing your exposure within the confines of your personal tastes and expectations.

2 STARTING OUT WITH LINKEDIN

Ready to roll? Break out your computer and push that power-button, it's Go-Time! Unlike many social media platforms, LinkedIn can be somewhat intimidating at first because of the professional nature it encompasses. Fear not, it's a great platform for engaging, learning, sharing and collaborating—the key is to be in it. As with so many opportunities, you cannot play if you are not a member.

SIGNING UP FOR AN ACCOUNT

So you're excited and determined to make this happen, right? Well it doesn't get any simpler than this: point your browser to http://www.LinkedIn.com and be prepared to spend less than two-minutes registering. Signing up is actually no more than the most basic process of entering the foundational elements of your profile, then securing it with your email address and password. Simply enter your first and last name, followed by your email address and a password consisting of six or more characters. Clicking the big, yellow "Join Now" starts you on your new journey.

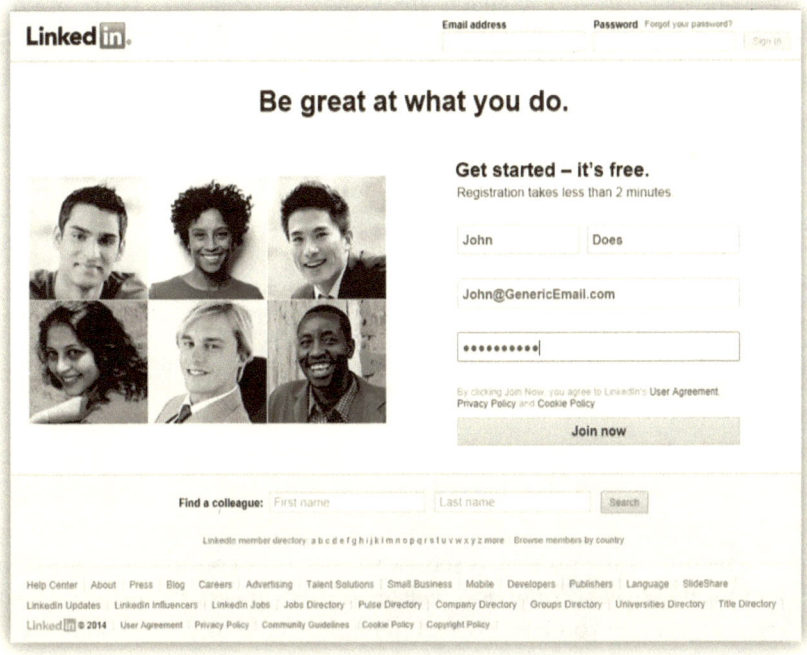

☐

From here, the newly registered user is asked to answer a few more demographic questions to establish their account and create their new profile:

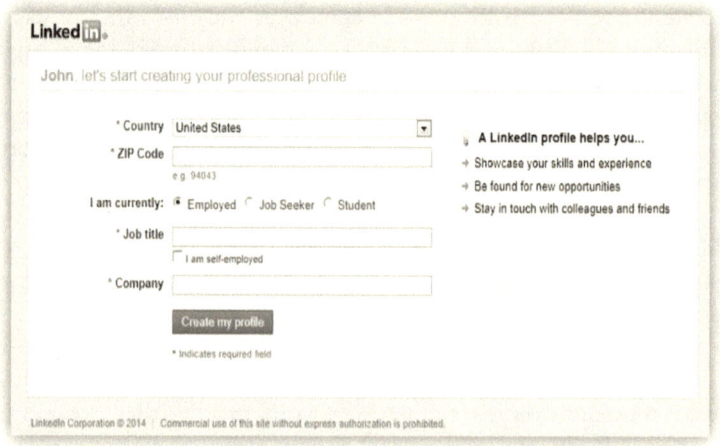

LinkedIn now offers you the opportunity to start growing your network right out of the gates by reaching out to the people you already know. Perhaps many of your contacts are already on LinkedIn. If so, the routine depicted below will allow you to synchronize with your address book (if supported) and start mining it for connections who can start building out your current network:

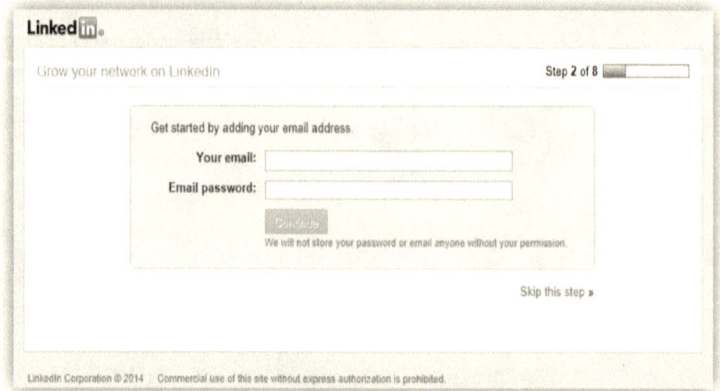

The rest of the process is self-explanatory. A confirmation email will be sent to the email account you registered from in order to establish that you are who you say you are. At this point, it is time to start building out your profile.

3 CONSTRUCTING A WINNING PROFILE

Your LinkedIn profile is like a short, engaging version of your resume. Notice I said—a version of your resume. After all, if someone wants your resume after reading your LinkedIn profile, they will obviously reach out to ask for it. Your goal is to engage someone who is searching for someone like you and catch their attention, then appeal to their inquisitiveness. You are best served by having the most complete profile possible. One can never know how a prospective searcher will come to find you. By using competitive keywords, engaging and attractive language, and taking full advantage of all fields available and relevant, you stand the best chance of being found by your target audience.

As well, there is no single recipe for the ultimate profile—it should reflect you and your targeted audience. As such, tailor it—and re-tailor it when you need to suit a particular audience. Tweaking your profile over time helps to expand your network by targeting different cultures, interests, segments and groups. Be clear and honest as you construct your profile—as your clarity will ensure the right types of people are attracted to (and link-up with) your profile.

PROFILE COMPLETENESS
There are five levels of profile strength on LinkedIn, and it will be annotated on your profile on the right side under the heading "Profile Strength":

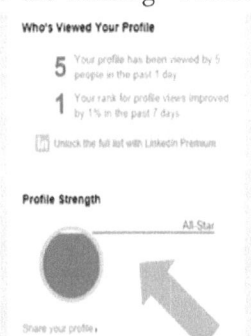

1. Just Beginning
2. Intermediate
3. Advanced
4. Expert
5. All-Star

Obviously, you want to be an All-Star—anything less is...well...less! To reach the All-Star level, you will need to have:

1. A Profile Photo
2. A Current Position that is Up-To-Date and Contains a Description
3. At Least Two Past Positions
4. At Least One Recommendation
5. Education Variables: At least one school, with dates attended, field of study, activities and/or societies. LinkedIn uses this to suggest new connections.

6. At Least 3 Skills: LinkedIn uses this variable to suggest endorsements and related skills to your viewers.
7. At Least 50-Connections: Upload your address book and review the connections suggested for you by LinkedIn to grow your personal network.

YOUR NAME

- Simple Enough – Write your First and Last Name. Add a Middle-Initial if it helps distinguish you from the pack.
- No clutter: Not the right place for acronyms, credentials, etc. This is also not the place for your company name.
- You are allowed to use up to 100-characters for this field

YOUR PROFILE PICTURE

When someone searches for you, a small thumbnail photo will appear next to your name and headline. For this reason, you need to bring the focus in to your head, neck and shoulders. If you go for a full-body shot, your features will be too small to be recognized.

- Do you need one? You bet—people whose profile includes a picture are 7-times more likely to be viewed than one without.
- This is for your headshot—not a wedding picture with someone else cut-out, no pictures with your dog, no cutesy cartoons, no family pictures, and no logos.
- LinkedIn is for professionals—save the fun stuff for Facebook. Use a professional-looking headshot with a neutral background that allows you to be the focus of attention.
- Remember to smile—this is about looking approachable, inviting and hospitable to future clients, prospective business associates, and perhaps future employers.

PROFILE HEADLINE

- #1 Most Important Feature of Your Profile! As such, it should be eye-catching, interesting, relevant and searchable.
- Keywords are important with your LinkedIn Profile—and your headline should contain the ones that matter. See "About Keywords."
- You can include LinkedIn Bullet-Points, Symbols, and Special Characters for a unique bit of eye-catching flair.
- You are allowed to use up to 120-characters for this field

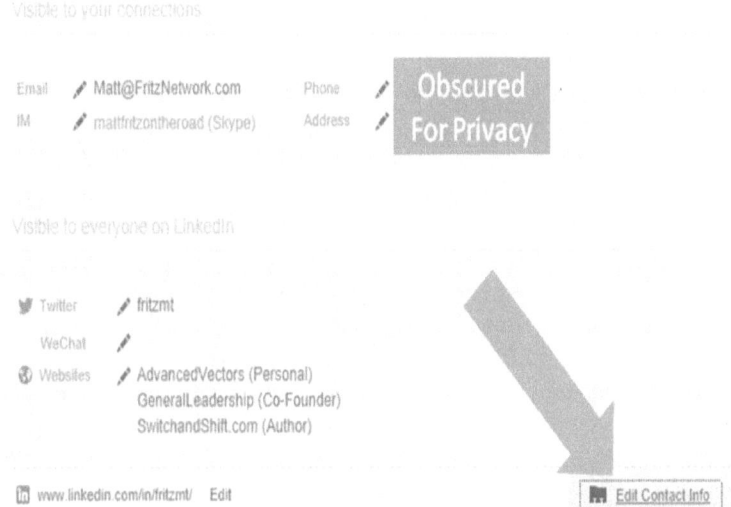

BONUS: CONTACT INFO SPECIAL FEATURES!

A little known connection opportunity comes from a relatively obscure little box that is hidden from view unless "Edit Contact Info" is clicked. This opens up a host of fillable-fields that can be displayed on your public profile:

You can list three websites in this section that you can brand to your needs. You can also affiliate your Twitter account, which can be very handy for those professionals who utilize this extremely valuable site. Twitter can be a wonderful way to express yourself and establish your personal and professional brand. If you've invested the time on Twitter, you can synergize this effort by linking your account here. I highly encourage you to tweet out "Link-Up with me on LinkedIn!" using an eye-catching picture and a link to your LinkedIn profile...you will be amazed how many find you!

Regarding your email, if you are in the market for connectivity in relation to a job or client search, then don't just list your email here and consider your job complete. You should make your email address stand out throughout your profile—weave it into different sections so that your viewers feel comfortable reaching out to contact you. Be clear—saying things like "I accept all invites to connect at me@here.com" or "Let's chat at me@here.com" invite your visitors to reach out and communicate with you. If the thought of putting your email address out there for the whole world makes you queasy, register for a special email address that you can use only for LinkedIn or other social-media exposure opportunities.

Since we are talking about email, why not add a link to your LinkedIn profile in your own personal email signature? After all, if you find creative and unique ways to splice your profile into your normal interactions, you are far more likely to create links with people you already know and expand your network in the process. Remember, the power of LinkedIn comes from your ability to leverage your existing network and expand into your contacts.

☐

SUMMARY

This is vital—you need to craft about 400-words highlighting your unique story. The words should be relevant and searchable. This section is designed to engage your profile's viewer, establish credibility, and let them know who you truly are. A viewer will spend about 5-8 seconds on your summary before making the decision to read further—so you need to hit them up front with an attempt to interest them IN YOU! There are many different ways to skin this cat, and it would be impossible to cover all of them. There are many specialty and personal service professionals who make a living by helping people author this very important section—in fact, some services can create your entire profile for you. Regardless of whether you choose to seek help or go it alone, it is best to fire up your word processor in a separate screen and spend some time writing this particular section with some intentionality (and maximizing the character count to your fullest potential). You can wisely use up to 2,000 characters for this section.

Basic tips are as follows:

- Avoid long blocks of information and maximize your use of keywords throughout your writing. Remember, search engines are reading this, too! (See "About Keywords.")
- Your goal here is distinguish yourself as a unique individual—not just one of the herd out there with skills similar to your own. As well, you want to make a connection with your reader that encourages them to spend some more time burning brain cells on you, versus the next person who comes up in their search.
- As this is your summary, do not write this in third-person. It's an appeal—a message from you about your #1 favorite topic...You! Nobody knows you better than you do, and this is your opportunity to tell your story. How did you find yourself where you are right now? What's your philosophy about what it is you do? What principles to you live by and why does that matter?
- Recall that you are writing this section for someone who has never met you. What would you want to know about yourself if you were meeting you for the first time?

- Don't cut/paste the summary from your resume here. If resumes are what your profile is all about, your goal is to entice the reader to actually contact you and ask for your resume. The resume is the second-step in your LinkedIn relationship...not the first.
- Make it attractive! Visual appeal is allowed—break it up, use LinkedIn Bullet-Points, Symbols, and Special Characters:, if appropriate.

SPECIALTIES

LinkedIn gives you the opportunity to spend up to 500-characters detailing the unique specialties you bring to the table. For this section, you should use only words or short-phrases, as opposed to sentences, to maximize your ability to slip in the keywords that will get you found when people are searching. In essence, you are speaking to more to a search-engine with this section, rather than a person. (See "About Keywords.") You have up 500-characters to spend in this section.

CURRENT AND PAST WORK EXPERIENCE

And so it has come to this—the meat of your profile. You can get as detailed as you wish—and you should be as detailed as possible—with the intention of utilizing those keywords you have developed. The more keywords you utilize in this section, the more targeted search results you are likely to appear in. (See "About Keywords.") Your most recent experience should be highly detailed, while older positions can be more succinct (especially those that are not relevant to what you are doing now). Again, eye-appeal is important here—so take advantage of special characters and bullets, if appropriate. (See "LinkedIn Bullet-Points, Symbols, and Special Characters" for more information.) You have the option to fill out the following fields as part of your work experience:

- Company Name: As you start typing in your company name, LinkedIn will pop-up possible matches for you to select from. This database of companies is taken from LinkedIn's "Company Profiles." As such, you may find that your company is not listed. Don't despair—you can always create a company page (if you are empowered by your organization to do so, of course) or ask your company leadership to consider creating a company page. By choosing a company from the selection list, you gain affiliation with fellow members of your team and allow your visitor to click on the company name to learn more about your organization, your fellow teammates, your products and services. If a logo is associated with a particular company page, that logo will display on your profile next to this position—which is nice way to break up the monotony.

- Position Title (100 Characters): Slowly enter the characters associated with your position title and LinkedIn will pop-up examples of commonly used titles. As we mentioned before, keywords are important. Entering obscure titles here will prevent you from being found in wide-net searches of LinkedIn members, which defeats the purpose of your profile. If you can utilize the choices which are presented. If your title is truly unique, however, type in your own and start a new trend. Someone else may be glad you created a new search-term for them to use for their own profile someday!
- Location: Slowly enter the characters associated with the geographical location of this position. LinkedIn will pop-up examples of commonly used locations. This is important, as it allows some uniformity in search routines. For instance, someone might be searching for someone exactly like you in the "Orange County, California Area" or in "Chicago, Illinois." The words you enter here allow you to be found when people do geographical searches for talent, clients and network connections.
- Time Period: Simply choose the month from a picklist and enter the year for your "From" and "To" periods. If you are currently working at this location, click the "I currently work here" box and the "To" period will be removed. Those organizations which you listed as "currently working here" will appear near the top of your profile. LinkedIn will also provide you the opportunity to update your headline, if you desire, from this entry.
- Position Description (200 Character Minimum to 2000 Characters Maximum)

VOLUNTEER EXPERIENCE

Share the causes you care about with your community. Doing so enhances your ability to locate new connections who share your interests. At the same time, lean out there only as far as you want your professional image to be impacted. Remember, future clients and employers may be watching—what do you want them to know about you?

PATENTS

Are you among the select few who have applied for and/or received a patent for unique creations? Wonderful—now share your fame! You cannot only tag yourself in this feature, but also those of fellow creators who collaborated on your invention. The connections you tag will receive a note informing them you mentioned them, and also giving them the opportunity to list the same patent in their own profile. Connections….LinkedIn is all about connections!

CERTIFICATIONS

In many industries, the certifications you hold are vital to your credibility. To be clear—you worked hard for them. List them out in this section, along with the issuing authority and dates. Why? Your mantra should be "Keywords!"

PUBLICATIONS

Are you a writer? Do you run a blog? Do you write for a magazine? Have you published a thesis, a novel, or a technical manual? This very important section has been made available so you can not only provide the title of your unique work, but also the source, the date, a short synopsis and…best of all…a link! If you co-authored a publication, give credit where credit is due by tagging your co-author. Like the patent-discussion above, they will receive a not kindly informing them of your gracious tag and allowing them to take credit for the work on their own profile, as well.

COURSEWORK

LinkedIn allows you to list the courses you took by title and course number, then tag them to the educational institution at which you gained the education. The schools you enter in the "Education" section will be presented to you in a pick-list you can select from for each course. Again, this feature is all about giving you keywords and affiliations from which to be found.

SKILLS AND ENDORSEMENTS

As in life, the skills you proclaim to have provide you limited credibility. The skills others endorse you for have real value—and LinkedIn is here to help. By listing out the individual skills and expertise you have obtained, you provide your connections the opportunity to share their two-cents on your abilities. Over time, certain skills will bubble to the top as "Top Skills" thanks to your connections endorsing you. This will become your brand—and highlight your expertise—to your viewers. It also provides a conduit for your connections to communicate with each other, as they are listed right there along with their recommendation. In total, you get to add up to 24-skills with up to 61-characters per skill.

EDUCATION

The true power of LinkedIn is found in the site's ability to provide recommendations for your network based upon your affiliations. Education provides a rich environment for finding people who share similar skills and interests for you to grow your network. The engine only works, however, if it is fueled by good data. Enter your schools and dates of attendance—even coursework—so that the database has a good picture of your educational history and connections. Don't be afraid to toot your own horn: enter any awards or honors you received as part of your education, as they greatly enhance your credentials! The courses you enter (see "Coursework" above) will be tagged along with each school, providing a nice, searchable cross-reference of keywords for your viewers to read.

ADDITIONAL INFO
INTERESTS
The data you enter here add to your keywords—and they become searchable. When displayed to your viewer, the words you entered are clickable search terms that search for other users with similar interests. You are given 1,000 characters to use for your keywords and terms.

PERSONAL DETAILS
If you enter your birthday and marital status here, it will be displayed to your viewers per your security settings. By default, it will only be available to your first-level connections.

ADVICE FOR CONTACTING YOU
The information you enter here will be visible to people who view your profile. This is especially useful if you want to make an offer to your viewers. An example might be, "Contact Me for a Free eBook" which provides an incentive for viewers to reach out and contact you.

HONORS AND AWARDS
This is a great section for you to list your accolades and achievements for your viewers to see. The honors and awards you choose to display will be tagged against a position, selectable from a picklist made up of your work experience.

ORGANIZATIONS
The information you enter here will be clickable/searchable by your viewers as a way to find people with similar interests. Again, these keywords might help you be found by someone searching for other members….like you…who are part of their club, group or organization. Separate organizations by commas to make each entry individually searchable.

PROJECTS
This feature allows you to increase your keyword exposure by adding project titles and associating the occupation (a picklist taken from your work experience entries), date, a URL and a description. You are also able to tag teammates who participated in this project with you, increasing your cross-network exposure and nicely letting others have the ability to add the project to their own profile.

LANGUAGES

Do you speak multiple languages? You can highlight your skills by entering different languages you speak, along with choosing a level of proficiency from a picklist. These keywords could be very important for someone searching for someone with just your skills.

TEST SCORES

If these keywords have value to you, take advantage of them by entering the name of the test you want to highlight, along with the occupation (selected from a picklist made up of your work experience entries), the date, a description and the all-important score.

MATTHEW T. FRITZ

4 GET OUT THERE!

A WORD ABOUT CONNECTIONS

A connection is made when two accounts are linked-together. To get the most out of LinkedIn, you will want to make as many connections as possible. Increase your numbers by inviting people who you know from sources you already have: your e-mail address book, your rolodex (do people still use those?), and your professional and education contacts. You can also use the "Find Alumni" tool from the "Network" drop-down menu to connect with the people you know at the educational institutions you entered. You can also use LinkedIn Groups as fertile fields for harvesting connections with people who share similar interests. (For more on this, see "Groups.") Above all—make your connection requests personal. LinkedIn's standard connection invitation is just that…standard. Take advantage of this opportunity to be personal and make a good first impression with your new contact. After all, that person is sharing their network with you!

Would you go to a social function with your business, walk up to a stranger with a copy of your profile, and loudly exclaim you would make their business dreams come true by helping them with their business? Surprisingly, that is what many people do virtually on LinkedIn via their attempt to invite people to join their network. Rather than cold-call people via impersonal spam messages inviting them to join your network—be personal. Each connection attempt is a transaction—and transactions are not all about you. Understand who your connection target is, what they might want from the relationship, and personally invite them to join your network in a respectful way. This is how you grow your connections in a meaningful and intentional manner.

How many is too many? That remains to be seen. It has been discussed that there is a cognitive limit to how many people you can maintain a stable social relationship with. This number, called "Dunbar's Number," suggests that humans can comfortably maintain about 150 stable relationships. Psychologists assert that numbers in excess of 150 in your social network impose extra rules and restrictions in order to keep your social group cohesive. Enter social media, where people define their environments by how many Twitter-followers they have, the number of Facebook friends they maintain, and the number of connections they cultivate on LinkedIn. The beauty of LinkedIn's networking feature is that it allows you to grow your network comfortably and sustainably…well in excess of Dunbar's Number. LinkedIn is not constrained by the need to constantly interact and engage with each and every member of your professional network to be effective. You reach out and connect with whom you need, when you desire, and the cycle is returned based upon the other person's ability. In short, LinkedIn provides an opportunity to expand your individual capability by leveraging a virtual rolodex of talent, interests, contacts and personalities to your mutual needs at the time of engagement. So grow your network, preferably in excess of 500 connections, to experience the maximum benefits available to well-connected members.

RECOMMENDATIONS

Believe it or not, prospective employers and clients use LinkedIn professionally to screen future candidates and prospects. It is sometimes intimidating to learn that your clients have done their homework on you via LinkedIn—and the face you show online is the face they choose (or don't choose) to do business with. Researchers see what you're up to, who you connect with, the groups you are associated with, and who has recommended you. As such, an effective LinkedIn profile takes advantage of the Recommendations feature. It is important for you to include as many recommendations—quality ones—as you can comfortably obtain.

It's a two-way street, so give as much as you receive. Building a bit of relationship-karma by providing a recommendation for a client, supervisor, or friend can go a long way towards strengthening your network. On LinkedIn, it's always as nice to give as it is to receive. Simply select any member of your network and view their profile. Hovering above their "Send a Message" button near the top of their profile, you will be presented a list of choices:

- View Recent Activity
- Suggest an Update
- Recommend
- Endorse
- Find Preferences

By choosing "Recommend" you have the choice to identify yourself as a Colleague, Service Provider, Business Partner or Student. Depending upon your choice of relationships, you will be provided the opportunity to share the relational basis (supervisor, coworker, subordinate) for your recommendation, as well as each of your respective titles at the time, and a written recommendation--which will appear on their profile.

GROUPS

LinkedIn success is about interacting and engaging with your contacts and making new ones on a regular basis. A great way to facilitate this is the "Groups" feature available to all members. LinkedIn allows you to join up to 50 groups—and you can even start new ones of your own, should you be unable to find one that suits your unique needs. Being a member of groups allows you to interact with other members who share similar interests, and helps show that you are an active contributor to the community. Don't be a virtual wallflower—get out there and find one that piques your interest. Engage with fellow members through thoughtful questions and polite dialogue. This not only builds your credibility, but also promotes your name and value to fellow members who can join your network.

From the "Interests" menu on your home screen feed, select "Groups" to be taken to the LinkedIn Groups interface. From here, you have the option of searching for groups that interest you and joining them. Not all groups are open for membership—some are closed and require a moderator to approve your admittance. Simply find the groups that interest you and click into their dedicated page. Once there, you have the option to join by clicking the "Join Group" button. Once you are a member, you can interact with other members and even seek a connection-link with your network.

You are allowed to join up to 50 LinkedIn Groups—and you should definitely do so. Us the LinkedIn Group Search Engine to scope out the ones that interest you based upon your own search terms. If you aren't finding what you are looking for, start your own group—you can start up to ten of your own (which count against your 50, by the way). Take advantage of the collaboration available within groups by using the boards (job and discussion), as well as messaging other group members. Do be courteous, however, as each group is its own little community. If you're the member who is constantly waving your hand in everyone's faces, expect to be "voted off the island."

ENDORSEMENTS

Endorsements provide members the opportunity to highlight skills and experience they believe are showcased in an excellent manner by an individual. For instance, when viewing the profile of an individual in your network, you may automatically offered the opportunity endorse that person for a particular skill which they have listed in their profile. Alternatively, you can choose to endorse a contact by hovering over the "Send a Message" button near the top of their profile and selecting "Endorse." You will be presented with a list of individual skills to endorse the member for, which you can modify to include areas of expertise the members may not have even listed for themselves. Over time, those particular keywords consistently endorsed more than others will percolate to the top of the member's list as "Top Skills" for all to see. This has the added benefit of forming a talent-brand for a person's profile, as well as facilitating simple communication among members.

FOLLOWING PERSONALITIES

The home screen feed is a busy place. Updates, articles, connections, and information will appear to you based upon the interests, skills, and contacts you identify through your membership settings and activities. Among these information feeds may be individuals who are well-known personalities who aren't necessarily a part of your personal network. While you may not have the opportunity to reach out to them personally via a connection, you may have the opportunity to "Follow" them—keeping the articles and information they publish in your feed. As well, the people you follow will be shared with viewers of your profile—which helps paint a broader picture of your professional interests. Want to be affiliated with someone famous or influential, but don't have the network connectivity to add them to your personal network? Following is the answer for you!

5 ADVANCED FEATURES

LinkedIn is not stuck in the here and now…it is constantly evolving to be more relevant to the ever-changing marketplace of data, humans and needs. As such, there are constantly new features being added which provide increased value to the community and external-searchers alike. For instance, you can now upload videos directly into your profile—along with links to documents, images and presentations highlighting your work. If it is relevant to who you are and the image you are attempting to project— take advantage of these features. On the flip side, don't damage your image by working overtime to use every available feature only to find that you are sharing substandard material that highlights a weakness of poor attention to detail.

A fully text-based profile is not a killer, but it also not something that stands out. Look for the (+) symbol throughout your profile-edit page so you can upload links to content you feel is important to your viewers. Items you upload will display with the title and description fields pre-filled based upon the content. Take the extra time to personalize these fields by editing the text and saving something that better reflects the content you are sharing. Shoot for visual-appeal by sharing content that catches your reader's attention and encourages them to learn more about you by clicking on the links. A nice-looking graphic helps to break up the monotony of a text-dense page, as well as sharing with your viewer valuable extra-information.

MOVE THINGS AROUND
If you see the little two-way up/down arrow in your edit screen, LinkedIn is giving you the opportunity to move things around. Simply grab the handle by clicking and holding on the two-way up/down arrow and moving the section or field where you want it. This is extremely valuable if you are trying to highlight something very important or relevant near the top of your profile page that you want your readers to definitely notice about you.

PRIVACY AND SECURITY SETTINGS
You will want to spend some time tinkering with your account privacy and security settings to personalize them to your preferences. Not every bit of information about you is suitable for everybody. Your goal is to find the ultimate balance between being found and keeping your personal information safe. For instance, some things just aren't meant for online consumption—especially if you have security concerns. Only you can judge

what is appropriate for sharing, and LinkedIn has a host of options available to customize your information display. Spend some time learning about the differences between your public profile (the display shown to the whole world) and your private profile (what your network sees). As well, you can change communication preferences, group memberships, and overall account settings. This is necessary for all users, and you will want to revisit this from time to time in order to tweak settings to suit your current needs.

Many settings are created by default—among them is the notification setting alerting your network when you make changes to your profile, make a recommendation or follow a company. You can control what people see by selecting "Privacy and Settings" from the drop-down menu off your small profile image in the top right, then selecting "Turn on/off your activity broadcasts" and deselecting the option to make automatic broadcasts.

EDITING YOUR PROFILE

Nothing you enter in LinkedIn is chiseled in stone. Don't be afraid to try new looks, or to tailor your profile for special events. Simply click on the pencil-icon anywhere in your profile edit page to initiate changes. To the right of your profile-edit page should be a dialogue entitled "Notify Your Network?" This selection turns on/off the option for LinkedIn to automatically post a network update to all of your connections that you've made a change to your profile that they might want to see. The option is yours to decide if, or how often, you want to show up in their information feeds.

WHO'S VIEWED YOUR PROFILE

Now that you're out there, you'll want to see how effective your effort has been. LinkedIn provides options to see how you are trending and to discover more about your viewers—where they work, live and what they do. You can see, to a degree limited by your membership-level, who has viewed your profile. This is valuable, since you can then reach out directly to people who may have stumbled across your profile and invite them to join your network. With all of this knowledge, you can determine the best ways to be discovered and receive more exposure.

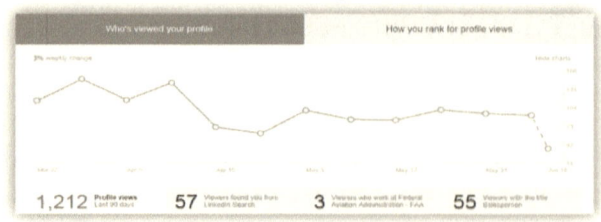

☐

BONUS: UNIQUE URL!

You can enhance your personal brand by creating a custom URL for your public LinkedIn profile. This is an extremely powerful statement to your reader that you have high situational-awareness. Rather than a profile URL that looks like something from a technical manual (http://www.LinkedIn.com/), you can have a professional looking (and easy to remember) URL that someone can reference later (http://www.LinkedIn.com/in/fritzmt).

To take advantage of this feature, click on the arrow to the right of "Edit" and select "Manage public profile settings":

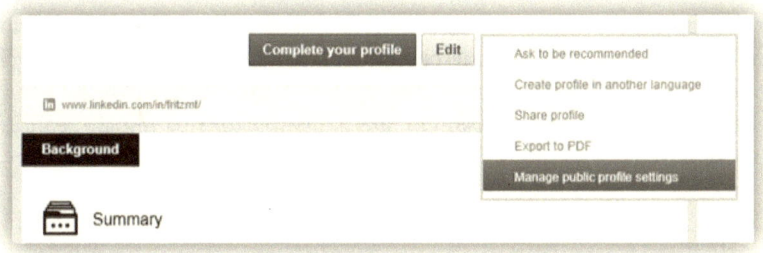

From there, search on the lower right side of your public-profile settings to find the dialogue that allows you to customize your public profile URL:

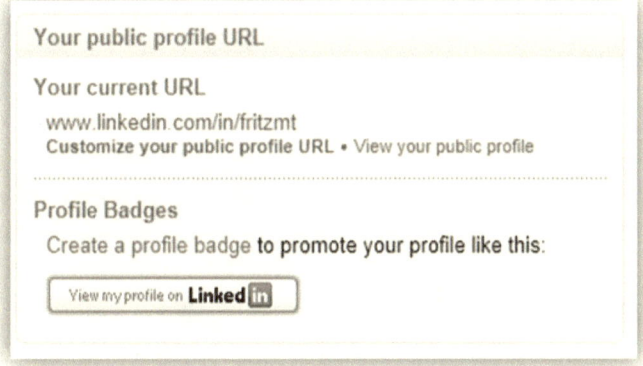

A popup should appear as follows:

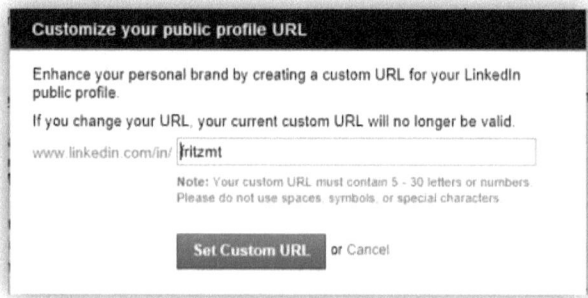

Select a URL that capitalizes upon your keywords. You have 30-characters to fill with something that is catchy, memorable and fits your profile. In my case, I chose "fritzmt" because it is small, simple and fits with my personal branding scheme. You can find me as "fritzmt" on Twitter, LinkedIn, Facebook, Wordpress, etc....consistency in branding is important to me. Whatever is important to you should be reflected in your intentional choosing of your customized URL. Tip: You cannot change your URL more than 3-times in 6-months. LinkedIn enforces a 6-month waiting period before you can change it again after this initial creation....so choose wisely!

6 THE PHILOSOPHY OF FOCUS

As LinkedIn is a diverse platform, so are its members. For this reason, there is no "one-size fits all" recipe for the perfect profile. Profiles are customizable in many different ways; as such, they reflect the personality of their owner. In fact, I would argue that having all members with the exact same profile look/feel would make the interface boring and uninspiring.

That said, there are some relevant statistics that indicate you have a better chance of achieving your goals if you follow certain conventions regarding the focus of your profile. For instance, why do you have a profile on LinkedIn? Are you looking for a job? Are you marketing your potential as a public speaker? The answer to these questions would lead you to very different profiles. If you were in the market for a job, then your profile would be built with the job-hunting focus in mind. You would be selling yourself for a certain position, industry, company or target group. If, however, you were merely providing an online profile to market yourself as a public speaker, then you—yourself—would be the brand. As you can see, the way in which you construct your profile can have very different outcomes and very different underlying factors. Here's the best part—you get to choose!

With LinkedIn's highly customizable profiles, you can drag/drop features where you want them. For example, you may want to move your Skills up towards the top where they can be found in a quick scan of your profile. Why? How long do you think a visitor to your profile will linger on your page to read all the way through the small novel you created about you? After all, you were going for keywords so you can show up in searches. Now the searcher has found you—and they're on your page! What do you want them to see first? Likewise, how do you want to draw your reader's eye to what matters? Bullet points, line breaks, and line-breaks help to cut through the monotony of a page and steer the reader to the things you want to highlight. In a quick-scan, your reader should come away with the most important information about you via the intent you have laid into the profile. Intentionality, after all, is the whole reason you are reading this guide.

ABOUT KEYWORDS

If you are familiar with the term SEO (Search Engine Optimization), then this topic will be no surprise to you. The LinkedIn profile is searchable in its entirety---that is one of the things that makes LinkedIn so valuable to people searching for talent and business. You should choose your keywords with intentionality—ensuring they are relevant to you and are the kinds of words sought after by people looking for someone like you. What good is it to be a truly great person with a truly valuable skill or service if nobody ever finds you because you used words that were so unique, they would never be found? This is where you need to do your research. Search for people who you believe are like you, or offer the products, skills or services you have to offer. Continue searching until you start to notice trends in the words bringing the people you want to emulate to the top of your search list. Those are the keywords you want to use to show up consistently in searches by the people looking for you.

Don't stop there! Once you've built your profile, log out, do a few test searches, and see if your name comes up on the list. If you are buried a few pages deep in the search results, you may want to make a few changes. LinkedIn is as much about being found as it is about making connections. Keywords ensure the audience you want to target finds you.

BONUS: LINKEDIN BULLET-POINTS, SYMBOLS, AND SPECIAL CHARACTERS:

- Stars: ★ ✪ ✲ ✩ ✪ ✪ ★ ☆ ★ ☆ ✵
- Arrows: ☛ ☜ ☞ ☟ ☞ ☝ ⇨ ► ◄ ► »
- Traditional bullets: ■ ♦ ◆ ●
- Ticks: ✔ ✗ ☐ ☑ ☒
- Email: ✉ ✍ ✎ ✏ ✐ ✆ ✇ ⌨
- Phone: ✆ ☎ ☏
- Symbols: ⊟ ▄ ■ ━ ▓ ░ ▒
- Hands: ☜ ☛ ☞ ☟ ☞ ☝
- Music: ♪ ♫ ♩ ♬ ♭ ♮ ♯
- Arrows: ← ↑ → ↓ ↔ ↕ ↖ ↗ ↘ ↙ ⇐ ⇑ ⇒ ⇓ ⇔ ⇕ ⇦ ⇧ ⇨ ⇩ ← → ↔
- Smilies: ☺ ☻ ⚫
- Zodiac Signs: ♃ ♄ ♅ ♆ ♇ ♈ ♉ ♊ ♋ ♌ ♍ ♎ ♏ ♐ ♑ ♒ ♓
- Cards & Chess: ♔ ♕ ♖ ♗ ♘ ♙ ♚ ♛ ♜ ♝ ♞ ♟ ♠ ♡ ♢ ♣ ♤ ♥ ♦ ♧

7 FINAL THOUGHTS

Thank you for allowing me to share my insights into what makes LinkedIn one of the most powerful networking tools in our social media environment. Through this platform, a diverse multitude of people is capable of gathering around common ideas. It is my hope that the insights provided in these pages prove valuable to you in your quest to be noticed, found, interacted with and connected.

It is worth noting that you don't have to go it alone when navigating these waters. Hosts of professionals are available to lend their expertise and helping hands to your effort. From resume writing to profile building, these experts are capable of leveraging their experience to provide you with a stellar profile anybody would want to read. In the end, the benefactor of the professional's talent is you...the subject of their muse.

Social media is a competitive environment, and there is significant competition among competing platforms for your business. As a result, the landscape is constantly changing. By the time you are reading this, it is quite possible LinkedIn has added some amazingly useful features not covered in this text. For this reason, I make myself available to you for a continued conversation. Look me up over on AdvancedVectors.com to pick my brain and ask any questions you may have. My father once told me an expert is someone whom you have never met and is from more than 30-miles away. The internet has the power to bring us all closer to one another—breaking down geographic boundaries and making miles nothing more than electrons. As such, rather than an expert, consider me a fellow traveler: eager to learn with and from your leadership ventures. If that venture takes you on a foray into LinkedIn, I am happy to be your guide.

Best wishes to you for continued success, growth, prosperity and fortune. Thank you for reading this guide!

ABOUT THE AUTHOR

Matthew T Fritz is a leader and mentor in the field of complex organizational change, emotional intelligence, and organization strategy. A successful DoD senior-acquisition program manager and test leader, Matt has earned documented success in the areas of test and evaluation, assessment, technology development and flight operations. He has specialized experience in cost, schedule and performance management and is an active duty Field-Grade Officer with command-experience in the United States Air Force. Matt is also a certified acquisition professional, as well as a certified Emotional Intelligence Trainer/Practitioner. He and his wife, Stacy, enjoy life with their daughter and son in New Mexico.

Look for Matt on LinkedIn at LinkedIn.com/in/fritzmt
You can also find him at AdvancedVectors.com
and GeneralLeadership.com